For permission requests, please contact the author directly at:
Loosen Your White Collar
Melissa Anzman
melissa@loosenyourwhitecollar.com
http://loosenyourwhitecollar.com

Contents

Introduction

- My Story
- Results Matter
- The Good Old Days
- The Solution
- Who Should Read This
- The Reality of Love at Work

INTRODUCTION

Hi, I'm Melissa Anzman and I'm a former Human Resources corporate drone turned founder and lead coach at Loosen Your White Collar. After spending more than 10 years in various HR environments and being frustrated with every job that I had along the way, I finally took the leap and left my high-paying corporate job to follow my own dreams. Now I help working professionals fall in love with their job (again) so they are able to live more fulfilled and balanced lives.

Have you ever woken up dreading getting out of bed and going to work, or perhaps you've had a perpetual case of the Sunday night blues. You keep trying different things to help you hate your job less or to make it at least tolerable, but all of your attempts left you feeling more trapped, completely disengaged or disgruntled, or feeling like you were destined to be miserable at work?

Me too - I've been miserable at work the past 10+ years or so. When I started my corporate career without a clue to what I wanted to do with my life other than climb the corporate ladder, everyone told me that all I had to do was get my foot in the door at a good company and stay there to gain seniority and credibility. I thought that if that advice worked for everyone else, surely I could make any job work… except, I couldn't. I quickly realized that I hated my job and landed a new one that was surely going to be better. The next job was not any better, so I found another job – and the pattern continued. One year in each position before I bolted to "greener pastures."

I had no idea how to break the cycle of Sunday night blues, especially when they turned into Sunday morning blues and eventually Saturday blues. It was awful – I went in search for answers, seeking solutions. Surely others before me hated their jobs and figured out a way to stay employed. So I talked to everyone I knew: new grads, people who have been in their jobs for 20 years and everyone in between. Their best answers all echoed "suck it up and just be miserable." Seriously? For as much time as I spent at work, redirecting my focus to my next incoming paycheck or all the bills I needed to pay, just didn't even out with the feeling of being trapped in jobs that I hated.

And the most upsetting part about it all was that even when I went to a new job, my problems and dread followed me there. My boss was a moron, the people I worked with were not nearly as efficient as they could be, I was always on call, and so on. I could not escape the things that were making me unhappy – even when I changed the variables surrounding the situation. Something needed to change drastically, I wanted to be content at work, if not downright enjoy it.

My Story

I knew that I was never going to make it in one job for any amount of time unless I figured out a way to beat the game. So I went back to all the people I talked to and asked even more questions. Being in Human Resources, I was able to capture unique insights from so many different employees – from line manufacturers to senior vice presidents; asking them things like what kept them focused, motivated, engaged – and what was influencing the opposite results. And from their experiences combined with my own (including a lot of trial and error), I created my own solution to help keep me, and my clients, in a state of love with their jobs. This was a work in progress for some time – I experimented with a few different jobs to make sure that my solution and exercises were sustainable and applicable, and above all else, created the work/life balance I was seeking.

Results Matter

Through applying everything that I learned, I was able to stay in one job for three years and a second job for four years – each a lifetime compared to my previous job-hopping hobby. But my own results are just one example of how you can fall back in love with what you do – my clients are the real superstars.

One of my clients, Kathy, came to me saying, "I hate my job, but since I'm so inexperienced, I am ready to be miserable at work for the next three years, since I have to." I literally screamed "NO, YOU DON'T!!!!!" when I got her email. Through working with her, she was able to not only overcome that kind of thinking, but she is now a top contributor at her job and looks forward to going to work every day – and folks, this was two years ago.

Another client, Gaby, needed to stay in her current job. As the breadwinner in the household with a new kid and responsibilities with a capital "R," she didn't feel as though she was able to just up and "follow her dream all willy nilly now." She felt trapped and burdened with more responsibility than I could even imagine, she wasn't able to spend enough time with her family, and she stopped doing the things she loved outside of work. Complete apathy. No one was happy – so we changed it! She stayed in her current job, received a promotion (bonus side effect – yay!), and restarted her creative pursuits outside of work. A win-win all around.

The Good Old Days

I assumed the old tried and true Corporate America formula could work for me: work hard, stay put, earn a paycheck. Hating your job is the norm. But it doesn't need to be like that anymore. There are so many ways to rebalance your love for your job. It's not an all-or-nothing pursuit. You can still stay in your current job and actually want to be there – or at the very least, not dread it. Maybe you're thinking of changing jobs further down the road, but don't want to hate where you're at while you're waiting. The same principles apply – YOU drive this bus, and it's time to embrace the many options that are available to us in today's working environment. Are you ready to join me?

The Solution

Six Steps to Fall in Love (with your job):

1. You Have to Kiss A Lot of Frogs
2. It's Not You, It's Me
3. First Date
4. Anniversary Celebrations
5. Lover's Quarrels
6. Happily Ever After (for now)

Who Should Read This?

This book will help you rewrite your love story with your job. If you feel as though staying with your current job makes the most sense, but you need to stop hating going there every day, this book is for you. While you may not currently love your job, there are still some redeeming qualities to it. Even a horrible job does not have to be dreadful. It's time to reconnect so you are able to capture some of the pizazz your job used to have, be happier while searching for a new gig, or be ready to buckle-in until it's time to make the big leap yet.

I want to help you get the most out of what you are already doing, while helping you shift your sense of obligation and dread into something that is meaningful and sustainable. Just like any matchmaker, there may be a few bumps in the road along the way, but stick with me, and I will be sure you land the perfect match.

This is not a magic love potion or a one-size-fits-all formula. Simply reading this book will help, but reading it alone is not enough. If you are ready to commit to working through the exercises included, and want real results to start living a more fulfilled and content life with work being a positive instead of a negative part of your life, then this is the book for you. Not committed. Not ready to dig deep within yourself. Please put this aside for the time being. When you have absolutely had enough, I will still be here waiting for you to help you fall in love with your job (again).

The Reality of Love at Work

I hate to break the bad news, but loving your job does not look like what the movies tell you. It is not an all-consuming fairytale of roses, fine wine and snuggles. Yes – enjoying what you do or "following your passion" on a daily basis does make it feel like less of a struggle for some people, but work sometimes need to be... well, work. For even the most jealousy-inducing jobs your friends have, there are always compromises and annoying things that pop up just to remind us we are at work. Just like any other relationship, it is all about finding the perfect balance for you – understanding what you need out of your job, and what you get in return.

Loving your job does not mean that you are gloriously happy in it at all times – but content. Contentment, or finding your individual balance and perspective, will help snap you back into a state of engagement and motivation to enjoy your current job. For some people, contentment may mean that you simply stop hating being at work; that when you leave work, work stays at work; or perhaps it means that you are open to exploring new and creative things at home because work is no longer weighing you down. Contentment is different for everyone, but it is a critical reality-check component for finding love at work.

And being in love means that you are always going to have good and bad days, there may be a few quarrels, but at the core – it takes effort to make it a success. And if you're willing to commit to the exercises within this book, you will find yourself energized when the alarm beeps in the morning, excited to get your work day started and have a new perspective on the true value you bring to the world.

Help Along the Way

At various points throughout this book, you will see HR Insider Tips where I provide you with some additional perspective about what happens behind the scenes in Human Resources. Look for the tie icon to find out more and to peek behind the curtain and learn about the potential "HR impact" from following these steps.

You Have to Kiss a Lot of Frogs

(Identify the Problem)

- Disharmony Dimensions
- Identify Yourself

You Have to Kiss A Lot of Frogs

When you reach a point of dread at work and absolutely everything annoys you, it is difficult to remember what made you miserable there in the first place. To start rebuilding the love, we need to identify the problems with your job. Each employee has a different experience and perspective, so what you hate about your job is not the same as what other people complain about. It is time to get down and dirty and be brutally honest with yourself – it is time to kiss a lot of frogs (and then do some kiss and tell).

Disharmony Dimensions

There could be many reasons why you are unhappy at work: your parking space is too far away from the front door, the paint colors on the wall, your budget keeps getting slashed, you have not gotten a raise in three years, or perhaps you are the only person who can form a cohesive sentence in the entire building. These are all (nit-picky) details that fall under larger umbrellas which I call Disharmony Dimensions.

#1: <u>Your Boss</u>

Hating your direct manager is a difficult situation to be in. He/she not only directs all of your work on a daily basis, but also usually holds the keys to your advancement. Hating your boss is not only normal, it is the main reason most people leave a company. So here is what is important to know: as much of a moron or jerk that your boss is, they are still going to be your boss (for now).

This disharmony dimension was at the top of my list in just about every single job I had (clearly there is a theme there). He/she was either incompetent, holding me back, less knowledgeable than me, kept track of my hours, or was technologically impaired. Needless to say, this was a consistent stand-out dimension in many of my jobs, and one that I needed to learn to cope with as he/she would remain my boss, regardless of what I thought.

Your boss is probably one of your disharmony dimensions if you are complaining about the following things:

- I am constantly teaching my boss how to do his/her job
- How or why does he/she have that position anyway
- If I get one more email from him/her, I'm going to scream
- I am sick of his/her micromanagement style
- His/her voice is grating on my nerves
- Why do I have to redo everything he/she does – ugh

#2: The Job Itself or the Tactics

We need to be very specific about this. There are so many aspects of a job to love or to hate. If you can't stand doing any job at your company, that is very different than being annoyed at doing expense reports (this is a tactical aspect of your job). It's time to live in the present – this is not about what your job description says or what you were originally hired to do – this is about what your current job truly is. And even more than that differentiation, are you dreading the job itself or the tactics?

You're most likely dreading the job itself if you are thinking or doing the following:

- I don't care about what I do – this is just so old already
- Who cares about getting anything done anyway – not even trying
- Your actions are not completed with integrity or regard of results
- I don't even know why I bother – someone else will handle it

Surprisingly perhaps, dreading your job itself is not as common as you would think. Even when you may not love being in a specific field or position, it is usually the job tactics that drive us to drink. The "job itself" misery presents itself as complete disregard of performance because you have had enough. You are spending your day doing nothing other than surf the web, or perform below standards without a care in the world. I'm going to assume that if you're reading this book, you are not quite at that level of despair or apathy… yet. There may be levels of the job itself that you do not like, but hopefully you are still ready to perform the basic duties.

Jonathan, one of my clients who worked in sales, came to me saying that he just hated everything about his job – basically at the point of giving up completely. When I asked him what about his job he hated, his response was, "I can't stand having to go to so many training sessions – it takes so much time out of my sales schedule; sorting through the tons of marketing materials to figure out which ones are most effective; all of the emails; generating daily sales reports." This was fantastic news! He still enjoyed being in sales (the job itself), he was just at his wits end with the tactics in his job. Luckily we were able to parse all of the tactics out so we could address them, all while he stayed in the job he innately enjoyed – sales.

Dreading the job itself is a horrible place to be, but fortunately disliking the tactics of your job is much more common. The tactics of your job include the expectations, the inefficiencies, the actual delivery, the daily tasks, structure, strategy, and so on. These are the things that we DO in our job – emails, interacting with customers, expense reports, travel, compensation reviews. Your day is filled with your job tactics, and these are usually the things that can get annoying.

Do any of these frustrating job tactics ring a bell?
- If I have to do X one more time...
- Why can't he just email me, why does he always need to call?
- How many levels of approval does a silly sign need?
- Is there a reason I need to file this report again?

HR Insider Tip

HR doesn't care how hard you work or how many hours you put in. In fact, if that's your excuse for needing a raise or less work, they are going to roll their eyes at you. All that matters is results – so if you feel overwhelmed with the demand, it is up to you to figure out how to make the situation better and lessen your own personal stress.

#3: The Demand

Being attached to your crackberry never leads to anything good. The pressure and demand of being always available, always reachable, always on, will wear you down faster than anything else. And the funny thing is, you created this sense of urgency and demand without realizing where it could lead. Your inner warning bells should be going off if you are feeling a sense of overwhelm by needing to be at work, checking your email at all hours, instantly responding to everyone, getting things done. You still care, but being in this state of "on demand" for too long will drive you right to your breaking point and beyond, if you are not careful.

If you are tired of feeling like you always need to "be on," if you sleep with your blackberry on your nightstand, if you are answering emails at 6 am or 10pm, if you feel like nothing you deliver is ever enough, then the demand of your job is a disharmony dimension for you.

#4: Idiots Around You

Ok, they are probably not all idiots, but they are definitely annoying. The people that you work with could be a big make it or break it deal for you. For me, I have transitioned from wanting the people I work with to be my friends (in my early days) to just people who sit across the hall with whom I interact/work with (now that I know better). Depending on where you are within that spectrum, the people around you could be the reason why you want to stay at your job, or why you want to leave pronto.

Those around you play a large role in your discontent if:

- Your coworkers are constantly wearing at your patience
- You feel as though you are the only one in the room who is qualified to do the job
- Hearing the conference call on speaker across the way is driving you batty
- You lose your patience repeating yourself over and over again
- You're not able to find one redeeming quality with at least one person

This is a huge blind-spot for most HR organizations – they are typically the "holders" of the company culture, but usually has no idea (or influence on) how it's actually applied out there amongst the people. In a strong HR department, they will be eager to seek your feedback and want to partner with you to implement real results for a better culture.

#5: The Culture/Environment

This category of annoyances encompasses all of the things about your company, the physical environment, the "culture" within your department and/or organization, and the expectations and standards. The way a company operates and its values can play a large role influencing your satisfaction levels.

Are the fluorescent lights above your work station getting you down? Or perhaps it's the weekly company-wide meetings. Maybe the desk in your area is not up to your standards, or the level of expected output for employees is unrealistic. The culture and environment are what makes your specific job at that one company, unique. It is about all of the little things you didn't know before accepting the position, that take some time to figure out from being at that company.

Sarah was one of my clients who was struggling a lot with her company's culture and environment. She moved into a smaller company from a large, conservative Fortune 200 company. She was used to having more than enough resources (such as office supplies, a lamp, the right desk chair, and so on), but was shocked to learn that she had to buy her own supplies if she had specific preferences, the office shared visitor chairs, and if she needed more light – it was up to her to make it happen. This was a huge culture shock for her and she was having a difficult time adjusting to the environment as it related to what she was used to. She was able to identify that the company culture plays a huge role for her at work, and we were then able to address all of her concerns.

#6: It's Me

This is a difficult one to cop to, but typically one of the top reasons. When we are dreading going to work, it's because something within YOU is not fully meeting your own expectations. This category is the leading reason of overall unhappiness at work – and it is the hardest category to own up to. It's time to look in the mirror and let all of the demons out. Don't worry, I won't tell anyone.

Your own personal expectations are a part of the problem if:

- You're not pleased with where you are in your career path
- You feel you're not being paid what you're worth
- You want your job to "be your passion" and it's currently "just a job"
- You're unhappy with an aspect of your life outside of work (think: relationship, money, housing, friends, and so on)
- You're questioning how did I end up here or why

Identify Yourself

Great – so now we know the most common reasons why our jobs suck. It's time to actually identify your problems. Work is required! Ready? Go!

While reading through the different Disharmony Dimensions, some of the examples or definitions probably resonated with you. We have all felt all of those things at one point or another, but you need to weed out the placeholders and figure out what the actual problems are.

Action Step:

For the next 30 minutes, bullet-out (a.k.a. – write down) all of the things that you hate about your job – big, small and everything in between. Do not move from your seat until 30 minutes are up (I'm watching you). You can write everything down on a separate piece of paper, or use this handy template.

Do not turn the page until you have completed your 30 minute brainstorm.

Ok, welcome back. Getting everything down on paper should make you breathe a bit easier, but we are not quite done yet. You have vented everything out, but you still need to identify the problem. Go back to the list of things you hate about your current job, and list next to your complaint the related disharmony dimension. Are you seeing any patterns or trends? Pick the top two dimensions to focus on for the remainder of this book (and then you can apply the tools you have learned to any other dimensions in the future).

Disharmony Dimensions:

1. Your Boss
2. The Job Itself or the Tactics
3. The Demand
4. Idiots Around You
5. The Culture/Environment
6. It's Me

My top two disharmony dimensions are:

_____ **&**

_____.

It's Not You, It's Me

(Shift in Mindset)

- We're Breaking Up
- Support Me
- Mourn the Loss
- The Shift
- Stop Hopping on the Gravy Train of Discontent

It's Not You, It's Me

Now that we know what's actually bugging you, we can start to make some progress to turn your frown, upside down. But making big life changes does not happen overnight – you know the old weight-loss saying that it took you a long time to gain the weight, it will take you just as much time to lose it all? Luckily for us, being happy at work does not take ages to change, but a significant change in YOUR mindset is necessary. And here is a little secret – the quicker you get on board with this step, the sooner you will love your job.

Now is the part where you are going to roll your eyes and ignore my well-earned advice and do things the hard way. You're going to try and skip this chapter because nothing is wrong with you – right? Skip the potential heartache and keep on reading. Learn this lesson the easy way for once.

We're Breaking Up

Have you ever gone through a heart-wrenching break up? Prepare yourself: you are about to go through another one. And this time, you are going to break up with yourself. In order to move forward and start to fall back in love with your job, you have to move past where you currently are with your relationship with your job.

And just like any epic break-up, it is time to mourn the relationship so you can start over again. Remember that this time around, you are not going through this alone – you have a strong network around you to support you, cheer you on, and even pick you back up when you fall back into your old habits – including all of us loosening our white collars.

Support Me

The first step to breaking up, is acknowledging all of the people in your close network who are either suffering due to your bad mood or are there to help you get back on the horse. If you have a significant other, I'm sure they are jumping up and down now ready for you to stop bitching about work. That one friend that you always complain to – she is on board.

Now that we know who is excited to help you shift your progress forward, it is time to make it official. When you say it out loud and share your journey, not only will it finally be real, but you will also be motivated to continue through knowing that you have people holding you accountable for your success.

Action Step:

Go tell your network that you are no longer going to hate your job. You are about to fall in love with your job again instead, and you need their help to keep you on track, tell you when you stumble, and enjoy a happier YOU when you've completed the process.

Mourning the Loss

You really are breaking up with your former self – with the person you were before you started reading this book. You need to commit to moving forward and acting from a more positive place of being. And just like any bad break-up, we need to mourn it. Why do we have to mourn something negative? You would be surprised at how attached you are to the person who has been unhappy. It has probably defined you, helped you fit in, given you a vent for frustrations, and allowed you to stay in the blame game. Any of that sound familiar? By committing to changing YOUR perspective, you are saying adios to your former self.

Your job is no longer your scapegoat. As we remove your job misery from the current equation in your life, it is going to feel uncomfortable. This is a life change. I'm going to help you break through several years (or decades perhaps), of malcontent, but you have to decide you dislike your former self, first.

Action Step:

Since you're going through a break-up, you need to go through those motions. Schedule a movie night with a tub of ice cream, go to a baseball game, tear something to shreds, or cry yourself silly. Do something to mark the end of your former relationship with your job.

The Shift

Guess what? YOU are the biggest problem in your current job equation. Of all of the variables in your work environment, you are the only component that can be changed right now. I know – but you're successful, and you are most definitely NOT the issue – it's the job, the company, your boss, etc., etc. No, it's not – it's YOU.

That sounds like a lot of finger-pointing – and perhaps you have your hackles raised or are rolling your eyes in my ridiculous accusations. I understand that – I was in that same state for TEN YEARS. I refused to believe that it was my perspective and mindset that was leading to a negative work environment. And even more embarrassing, I was leading others down that same path. It's unacceptable – and you deserve better. I urge you now: do not let ten years pass before you truly work on this step. Ok… coming down from my soap box.

There may be many aspects about your job that are frustrating, annoying, and perhaps even downright hostile. These "things" are the symptoms of your own discontent, manifested. But before we work on the situation and "things" that are getting you down, YOU are the puzzle piece that needs to be updated.

One of my favorite coaching moments is when one of my clients, Josh, realized that this was, in fact, true for him – he had a "light bulb" moment! He said (and I'm quoting here), "Wait – whoa. I am actually creating these problems for myself, aren't I? Holy s*%&! If I focus on my own reaction and things within my control, I actually have influence. Insane – I feel like I've been spinning my wheels. Why didn't anyone tell me this sooner?" I chuckled a little, on mute of course, because this was something we had been talking about, but he had not yet done the pre-work above. He was not yet ready to shift his mindset until that very moment.

STOP Hopping on the Gravy Train of Discontent

Being around other people who are unhappy at work is the easiest way for you to fall into that same state of unhappiness or despair. You need to separate yourself from your coworkers a bit, especially when it comes to engaging in office gossip. This will be an odd venture in the best office environments, and lonely and somewhat isolating in most others. But this is necessary to help you move forward.

Start setting some boundaries with your colleagues, subtly. If you are out to lunch and they start complaining about their boss, the company, or someone – politely change the subject. If they proactively seek you out to commiserate with you, remember a meeting/ email/client that you must absolutely address immediately, or, if you are bold, let them know that you're sorry, but you don't have time to gossip right now.

Over time, it will become clear that you are no longer a "go-to" person for commiseration and negative talk – which is fantastic! You may not know everything that is going on around the office – who is doing what to whom, but you will have removed yourself from the bowels of the negative environment. And after the left-out feeling subsides, you will realize how much lighter you feel. Carrying others' complaints and negativity is draining – remove this burden and you will be amazed at how easy it is to feel positive.

From my experience, there are more gravity issues in HR than in any other group – and sadly, they are typically the first group to throw their hands up and say "it is what it is." I don't necessarily agree with that approach, but look to HR to learn how to let some of the gravity issues you come across roll off your back. You will find it also provides you with the ability to have the real issues add actual impact /value – and HR can be a great ally when you bring them a problem/solution outside of gravity issues.

Gravity Issues

One of my former bosses was very pragmatic, which of course meant that I was rolling my eyes often. But one of the most important things I learned from him was something called gravity issues. He would say, "That's a gravity issue" at least three times a day. I was annoyed by the repetition and finally asked what that meant. He explained that, within a work environment there are certain things that, regardless of what you do, just cannot or will not be changed. Just like gravity is a constant, these "things" are constants. Holy golf balls, Batman!

Once you realize that there are indeed gravity issues at work, you will be amazed at how many of them you will run up against each and every day. Your current boss – that is not going to change right now; the company's values – gravity; your CRM system – it's staying; the organization of the company – not even on their radar to update; the people you work with – they will still be employed tomorrow. Get it? And just like gravity, if you are not able to impact the situation or change it for your benefit, why would you continue to be frustrated about the situation?

Talk about a shift in perspective, huh? Going back to your disharmony dimensions, which ones are gravity issues for you? If no amount of effort, work, concentration, banter, begging, pleading, or wishing will change the essential outcome of the situation, then it is time to move them off of your list of complaints and start accepting gravity.

Mantra as a Reminder

Unfortunately for us, changing your mindset is not a "one and done" action. You will get off track. Or, if you are anything like me, you may need to remind yourself about it several times a day. So create a mantra to help keep you in the right frame of mind – I couple my morning mantra with a fun song and dance at my desk (no one can see me… I hope). The important thing to remember is that you are working at change – and you need to remember why you want to fall back in love with your job.

Mantra suggestions:

- I, alone, will influence my mindset today – and I want to be happy.
- How can I surprise myself today through my actions, grace and patience?
- Work smart, not hard today.
- Don't sweat the small stuff, or the gravity stuff – concentrate on where you can influence today.
- I work to live, not live to work.

Figure out what works for you and make sure that you keep it on a post-it note close by at all times.

Pick a day and go.

It is time to pick your break-up (quit) date. No, you are NOT quitting your job outright or quitting smoking, but you should approach your shift in mindset similarly. You are officially going to break up with your former self and commit yourself to a new relationship. You are no longer the person who loathes your job, who engages in gossip, who loves nothing more than pointing out all of the negative things that surround you. You are kicking this habit.

It does not have to be a Monday, in fact, the sooner you can pick a date, the better. You will not be perfect, I'm not asking for cold turkey, here. You are allowed to stumble along the way, but in order to do that, you need to start. Pick now.

What's your break-up (quit) date?

_____

First Date

(Values)

- Let's Go Out
- Picking Your Outfit

First Date

Being ready to change your mindset is the first step, but remembering who you are and why you want to be happy at work sets the stage for a perfect first date. Understanding your values, what makes you tick, and what keeps you motivated is critical for your journey. Without having a clear sense of what is important to you, your efforts can be easily forgotten.

There are so many ways you can determine your values and what's important to you. Check out this list of almost 150 values by Steve Pavlina. While ideally you would look through the entire list and figure out which ones speak to you or perhaps complete a balance wheel, there is a quicker way for our purposes. And that's where our dating will begin.

First Date

Imagine you are going on a first date with someone who you have never met before. What needs to happen during the date to make you want to say yes to a second one? For me, I would need to laugh, have engaging conversation, feel comfortable, some attraction or intrigue, and enjoy his company. We all know when the first date will absolutely NOT turn into a second one. The same is true about your values and motivating factors.

Let's pretend for a minute that you have completely given up on your current job and are determined to find your perfect dream job at the most amazing company. How would you know when you found the one? Would your pay be ridiculous? Would you be leading a team of high-achievers? Could you work from home;? Would be surrounded by people your own age? Dream the dream right now and determine what things you would be seeking out in a new job (oh, and write them down).

All of these "things" that you would use to determine if a job or company is ideal, are important to addressing not only what has led you to fall out of love with your job, but will also help us determine what you need to change to make your current one better — what I call your personal balance scale.

Picking Your Outfit

Looking at your list of what your dream job would have from a values perspective, you will need to focus on the top two items. Do not freeze up here because you think that your top two are shallow or paint you in a bad light or you just cannot choose only two. No one is judging you for what drives you and what will help you show up each and every day. Your two motivating factors will most likely not be the same as the people around you. These are the things that you look for on a first date (or perhaps when you are interviewing) with a job – and it has also led you to hating your job in the first place. When you are not being driven by something, or you are not honoring the core of who you are, you will not be able to find joy and happiness by just showing up.

Think back to the reasons why you accepted your job in the first place. What attracted you to the opportunity? Also, what are the reasons that you have continued to stay there even through you are unhappy?

Here are some of the most common motivating factors or values to help you ponder:

- Money
- Authority/decision-making power
- Position, title, reputation
- Stability
- Learning new skills
- Freedom (of anything)
- Coworkers or clients with whom you get to interact
- Office environment or culture
- The job itself
- Impact or value added to the world – aka, meaningful work

Let's get ready for this first date then – what are the two "items" that would be at the top of your list when finding your perfect job match?

This is your first outfit, feel free to try on a few different variations and combinations that feel best and are sustainable. In other words, what are two different values that you can either keep balanced in your current job, or will allow you to flourish when one of the values significantly outweighs the other?

My first outfit looked a little like this:

- Motivation Factor/Value # 1: Really Interesting Work
- Motivation Factor/Value #2: How Much I'm Getting Paid

This was a great first date outfit for me when I'm looking at corporate jobs or what helped me stay in all of my previous jobs. After going on that date, for over ten years, I now have a different balance scale:

- Motivation Factor/Value # 1: Really Interesting Work
- Motivation Factor/Value #2: Freedom

You may need to think through several scenarios before you come up with your perfect fit, but realize that your motivating factors may be different depending upon the environment/field. In Corporate America, how much I earned was important to me – I was not ready to sell my soul for nothing. However, being a solopreneur, and in life in general, I'm not driven by money – it is more about being able to make my own choices, decisions and live creatively.

Be very clear and honest – what motivates you in your current job situation. What would you be willing to "put up with" or perhaps let slide, in lieu of something else?

Anniversary Celebrations

(Goals)

- Check-in Date
- Motivate Me Goal
- Celebration

Anniversary Celebrations

We are officially an item if you have made it this far – congratulations. But we still have some work to do! If you are anything like the employees I've encountered throughout my career, you moan and groan each year when you are required to create goals for your position. There is a reason why goal setting and performance reviews are a critical component to the working world – goals help you stay on track and focused along with an objective measurement of success (in theory).

Now we are going to apply the same goal-setting principles to your own life – and it is way overdue. Before we actually set any goals, you need to know what a true goal is. They are SMART – specific, measurable, attainable, realistic, and time-bound. Creating SMART goals take some time and practice to master, but are powerful when done correctly. You are going to set personal goals to remind you to celebrate each anniversary along the way.

Check-in Date

Not typically a goal setter? Not to worry, these will be more applicable than any goal you have ever set. The first and most powerful tool that I have learned along my own journey is to set a **check-in date goal**. Your check-in date goal should be a short-term goal, no more than three months out, in which you will fully commit to the following:

1. **You will be fully present in your shifted mindset from being miserable to falling back in love.**
2. **You will be committed to your current job. All talk, thoughts, discussions, or what-have-you's, about changing jobs, finding something else, quitting, or bellyaching about your current situation will cease. Alternatives have been removed from the situation altogether.**
   Remember: quitting your job is like a divorce, which is exactly what we are avoiding.
3. **You will track your goal date in plain sight, every day.**

How do I know this works? I was once in a situation where I was tied to a company through a contract – if I left the company before the contract was up, I owed the company a ton of money. I knew I had commitment issues when I signed the contract, so I saved all of the money just in case. But it would still be a significant blow to my personal bottom line if I had to pay a lot of money to the company that made me miserable. So I set myself mini-check-in dates to help me make through the entire contract. Here was my approach:

Goal 1: I committed to the above three things and gave myself permission to then reevaluate whether or not I was going to be able to stay following my goal date. All I had to worry about was the first goal date, and doing everything in my power to stay engaged and in the positive mindset throughout that time. By taking the option of leaving my job completely off the table, I was suddenly lighter – I did not have to worry about paying back a huge sum of money, I wasn't pondering the job market, I wasn't updating my resume or putting my feelers out there. I knew exactly what I had to concentrate on and did just that. To keep track of my goal date, I kept it in two places. In my old-school day planner, I had the number of days in a countdown fashion, listed on each day (writing that down in the first place was so fun!). The second way I kept that in front of me was through my wall calendar up in my office. Each morning when I got to work I took the fattest black sharpie marker and crossed out the day. The pleasure that simple act gave me along with the constant visual reminder that my goal date was getting closer, made me giddy. When my goal date arrived, I took some time and considered where I was, if I was able to commit to the same things as before, and determined my course of action – I continued to set mini-goal dates until I actually met my contract deadline! And I did it with a smile and less misery than I had the year prior in that position.

When you have something achievable to look forward to, coupled with an attainable date, perspective, clear direction, and a commitment, your mind settles into what is to come. Just remember that your check-in date needs to be SMART.

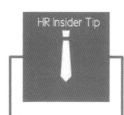

HR Insider Tip

How cool is it to take HR's own tools (and the agony and moans that come along with corporate goal-setting) and use the tools against them?

SMART Goals

- **Specific:** I will be fully committed and engaged at my job (if you want to get more specific, talk about what engagement looks like for you).
- **Measurable:** I will be in XX gear (more on this later); I will be content X% of the time; and so on
- **Attainable:** (this is usually understood by the commitment piece – can you be engaged, heck yes – it's up to your mindset)
- **Realistic:** Pick a date or expectation that is realistic to measure and to accomplishment; for example – being 100% committed all of the time is probably not realistic if you hate your current job, but aim for 90% - you can
- **Time-bound:** The goal date

Putting it all together: I will be 90% committed to contentment and engagement at my current job through August 31, 2012.

What's your first SMART check-in goal?

_____

Did you share your goal with someone? Preferably someone you do not work with– trust me on this one. Having goals is fantastic, but they only become real when you tell a friend. Be sure to do that. If you do not feel comfortable telling one of your friends or family members, not to worry – that's what I'm here for. Send me a quick email letting me know what your check-in goal is, and I will be sure to keep you on track and hold you accountable.

Motivate Me Goal

We have already learned what makes you tick and what is important to you in a job. Let's use this to our advantage and create a goal not only to help motivate you along the way, but also to keep your motivating factors in the forefront of your consciousness. This goal will give you something to achieve, versus something to look forward to. Just like the opposites of yin and yang, your check-in goal is your push goal – what you are heading towards. This goal will be your pull goal – what you will seek out along the way. You need both to stay balanced.

The geeky HR person in me will always suggest that your goals be SMART, but for this one, I want you to focus on the experience more than the technical goal itself. Here are some example goals based on the motivating factors and values we discussed.

Money

Money may seem like it is somewhat difficult factor to influence, particularly within a corporate environment. But if you are money-motivated, then this is a great challenge to take on during your check-in period. Some goals could be how to increase your income by $5000 or 3% within the next three months; start a side hustle to bring in $X during your time period; receive one spot award for outstanding performance; and so on. The main point is that you need to be creative in figuring out ways to increase your income either presently or within the near-term to help balance your money motivation. Your actions and interactions with others should have this goal in mind. A few warnings with money-related goals...

- You may not have the power or influence to increase your salary, keep that in mind if you do not receive it
- Be cognizant of how you are perceived while pursuing this goal. It's very easy to come across to others as single-minded, pompous, or a jerk. Money makes people uncomfortable, so be sure you have sustainable results while pitching your value
- This is more about the act of pursuit than necessarily receiving immediate returns – you are not entitled to anything

Authority or Decision Making Power and Position, Title or Reputation

Usually when we think about authority, we think of the person at the top. Well, that is not a realistic scenario to change overnight. But there are so many things you can track towards while working on your check-in date, and people tend to forget the many options in between. You can seek out mentoring opportunities (to be the mentor) at your company or local organizations; informally become a leader on your team; focus on one project or task and perform it at such a high level, that you earn the decision-making power and trust from your boss – and then ask if it can be transitioned over to you going forward; be proactive – is there a project or activity that will add a ton of value to the organization that no one has the capacity to take on? If you are spearheading it from the ground up, you will have the authority. Be a leader – even if you do not currently have direct reports.

These goals are about your mindset and seeking out opportunities where you can exhibit and apply your authority. That does not mean you are limited to "official" positions of authority – it is about what opportunities you carve out for yourself and what the perception of you is. Perception equals reality – so you may not be promoted into that position during your check-in period, but do this right and you will be on everyone's radar for all of the right reasons, going forward.

Stability

The act of being stable is a bit difficult to measure or create goals around since it's intangible. But if you are driven by the comforts that your consistent paycheck or company-paid benefits provide, you must continue to seek out ways to enjoy these benefits and turn the stability into an experience. Your company has many more benefits that you even realize – have you spoken to HR to review all of your options; have you visited the zoo with your discounted company pass? Do you fully participate in the 401k? Make it your goal to know everything there is to know about the company's offerings – and use them. Part of working in a "stable environment" is all of the perks along the way. Do not take these things for granted, they are a huge part of why you are there.

Coworkers or Clients You Interact With

The people you are surrounded by can make a huge impact on how quickly your check-in date comes. Now that you have stopped gossiping with them and started being a positive influence, you can work on enhancing your relationships with those around you at work. Have a consistent day that you lunch with people. Or perhaps schedule an after-work happy hour and invite people outside of your typical group – expand your horizons a bit. If you are traveling for work, see if you can partner up with someone new. These goals should be based around experiences and interactions with your peeps – so think big, think often, and consider impact. Maybe you only get to interact with people during lunch – how can you create new opportunities to bring people together? Are you involved in a company club or group? Can you start a club or group? Be sure to surround yourself with positive people and focus on how to bring them together as often as possible.

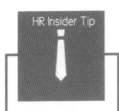

Learning New Skills

Most companies have many opportunities for you to grow and learn, particularly in larger companies. The catch? You have to drive the bus. Have you checked out all of the offerings that the Learning and Development group provides? Have you asked your boss to attend a conference or offsite class to help you enhance a skill set? Goals for this value should be around moving yourself forward. What skills do you want to learn during this time period; what knowledge will move you forward in the future; how can you best take advantage of the knowledge at your fingertips? Signing up for a course and attending it is the first step in creating a goal like this, but challenge yourself further by indicating how you are going to apply your new skills or learnings. And the great thing about these goals is that they are limitless. There is always something new out there for you take on and explore, it is simply up to you to take advantage of them.

Freedom (of anything)

Freedom is more about your frame of mind than anything else, but you can always try and carve out the feeling of freedom if you feel burdened in your current environment. Some great goals that increase your feeling of freedom at work include: creating an unique environment in your cube that makes you feel more free; take a mini-vacation – aka, splurge and use one of your vacation days to do something that you want to do; ask if you can have flex hours or perhaps work from home occasionally; make sure your attire is representative of YOU every single day; pick a project and do it your way – not necessarily the in-the-box way you've been conditioned to do it in the past.

More than anything, creating goals to help you achieve more freedom requires constant check-ins with yourself. No one, and I mean no one, will be helping you obtain additional freedom, so it is up to you to insist upon it and create it yourself.

<u>Office Environment or Culture</u>

To be honest, some culture issues will fall under the gravity scope. But that does not mean that there are not things that you can still do to impact your own environment or culture. I would start with thinking about what bugs you the most or what is missing in your current situation, and have goals surrounding those things. Or focus more micro – what can you change about your work space to make it more enjoyable – redecorate, change out the lights, add some personal touches? Have you connected with Human Resources to discuss your thoughts and offer your help? This is the time to move your complaints into action, without excuse and without settling into the thinking of "why should I be the one?" It's time for you to work towards changing your environment and culture to help you focus on what is most important to you.

<u>The Job Itself</u>

If you love what you do (or perhaps it's what you are supposed to be doing in theory), start going after it full force. Take pride in every action that you do and make goals around how you can elevate your job to the next level. What is missing, what can be more efficient, what needs to be tweaked, how many new ideas can you take to your boss? Are you doing absolutely everything you can to make the most out of what you do on a daily basis? Have you removed the things that are not really a part of your job? The biggest hurdle with this factor is to be sure that you do not get complacent – it is no one else's fault if you are not feeling the love with the job itself, you need to push ahead and figure out what you can like about it and how to play it to your strengths.

Meaningful Work

This motivating factor is quite easy to impact – who knew, right? You do not need to be curing cancer or saving puppies to find meaningful value in what you do day in and day out. Focusing on goals that allow you to recognize and/or drive more value to the people you are already serving can take you a long way towards your check-in date. Can you create or be involved in your company's philanthropy group? What can you do in the community with your coworkers to expand your reach and impact? Does your company recycle? Have you focused on the value that you bring to those around you every day? Meaningful work is about what is meaningful to you – not just building water wells or saving lives. It is critical to reframe meaning for you, especially if you are unable to find significant outcomes or value in your current role. How *YOU* can make an impact to others is what is important – change is made one small step at a time, so please stop pressuring yourself to make big sweeping world-changes on a daily basis.

My motivate me "pull goal" is:

_____

_____

Celebration

Now that you have at least two main goals, you need to celebrate each step towards progress – that's what anniversaries are about (phew – we made it another year; or let's never go through that year again). Either way, celebrate each step along the way on your path to fall back in love with your job. My favorite celebrations included a massage, dinner with friends at a nice restaurant, or a baseball game. As long as you are acknowledging both the good and the bad, you are marching forward to success.

Lover's Quarrels

(Bumps in the Road)

- Have You Learned the Lesson
- Downshift
- Boredom Has Taken Over
- Boundaries
- Be Five Years Old Again
- "Find Your Passion"
- Fight Fair

Lover's Quarrels

You and your job are going to have bad days. Just like any love story, there are going to be a few bumps in the road. You will learn more about yourself on these few bad days, than all of the days in between – and that's a good thing. Falling in love with your job is not a light switch that you can flip and it automatically stays on forever. So it is critical that you set yourself up for success and be prepared to address the roadblocks when they happen.

Have You Learned the Lesson?

Make this a game of sorts – when you are having a miserable day at work or something happens that annoys the heck out of you, ask yourself: What is the lesson? I am a firm believer that you will keep butting up against the same frustrations and situations until you have fully learned the lesson that is meant for you to learn – it is the universe's way of telling you that you will need that skill set further down the road. It is not easy to fully embrace this concept while you are trying to manage an unruly boss or a ridiculous travel schedule, but there is always a nugget to take away from each situation. Take some time to ponder the question thoroughly and be sure that you have a solid answer before starting to get back on track.

I remember being so annoyed with one of my former bosses who used to refuse to email anything. He would not answer questions, provide direction or forward on updates. Every email from him said and I kid you not, "Swing by my office to chat." Are you freaking kidding me?! Just ANSWER the email. After being frustrated to the point where I was considering looking for another job, I asked myself again: What is the lesson? For me, there were several lessons wrapped around that one trigger point – patience, learning how to interact with others in a way that matched his/her own preferences (a.k.a. – changing my approach accordingly), and being very sensitive of what is put in writing. Here's the thing – those lessons came in handy, particularly when there was an email leak that ended up with unscrupulous information on the front page of *The Wall Street Journal*.

The lesson that you are supposed to be learning may not be apparent in the moment, and you may need to have the lesson smack you upside the head several times before it finally seeps in, but there is a lesson within the madness. So make it your mission to better yourself and learn from the things that drive you batty.

Downshift

One of the requirements for getting my driver's license was that I needed to know how to drive a stick-shift. At the time, I had no idea how relevant that concept would be years down the road when I was working, but it is an invaluable tool that I learned too late in the game.

Downshifting: downgrade your efforts, responsibilities, responsiveness, and capabilities for a short period of time to get back on track.

Downshifting at work feels a bit like you are being naughty – and if you are an overachiever by nature, it will take a lot of reminders and convincing to make the downshift, stick. I had to constantly visualize the act of downshifting while driving, from fifth to second gear. You have most likely created unrealistic standards of performance and delivery for long-term sustainability. And nothing can throw you off more than having just one too many things to do, that very minute.

It is time that you reset your boundaries, even if it is just for a short amount of time, and work at the level of a good employee instead of trying to kill yourself to be a superstar.

Next time you are at work, I want you to look around and "review" your coworkers – are all of them delivering at the same level as you? Let me let you in on a secret – there are only a handful of key talent employees within a company, true superstars. Most of the work that gets accomplished is done by what you would consider "average workers."

I am not saying to stop doing work or underperform, but I am giving you permission to step off the gas pedal and work at a different level. If you are a three seconds or less email responder, up your response time to five minutes – or go even more drastic and only open your email once an hour (ask yourself: does the world stop turning when Larry does not respond right away?). If you are missing family functions to check your Blackberry, turn it off for a few hours after work. If you volunteer to take on every single project, stop volunteering – or only request to work on every other one. The biggest lesson you will learn when downshifting, other than being gloriously happy that you have some breathing room, is that *people will not notice – at all.* And remember, the most successful employees are those who are able to flex their efforts and output according to company needs – so start applying that in both directions, particularly when you hit a rough patch.

"But Melissa," you say, "how can you suggest I work less when I've already taken on the work of five people in this horrible economy?" That is exactly why you need to downshift! If you continue at the pace that you are and soak up all of that pressure, you are going to burn out. Period, end of story. I am not saying that you should stop working, stop contributing, stop adding value to your company – simply give yourself permission to take a breath every now and then and start reestablishing new boundaries at work.

Boredom Has Taken Over

Not having enough work to do can be a real struggle. You have to be in your cubicle for at least eight hours each day struggling to "look busy," while trying to feel as though you are contributing value at work. Being bored gives you ample time to steep in your unhappiness – a big no-no when we are working at falling in love.

The best way to bust boredom is to find something worthwhile to focus your efforts on. For me, I busted boredom by working on my side hustle (shhh – please do not tell my former employers). I was very careful not to use company resources, but I did use my time wisely by getting blog posts, ideas, and concepts down on paper.

Having some time on your hands provides you with "bonus time" to figure out your passions, explore new projects, and offer your expertise to other departments in need of an extra hand. In fact, being available for other groups can greatly impact your value perception at the office. And trust me, there are always departments looking for an extra hand. I used to help a Marketing group with trade show packets, IT with troubleshooting, and Public Affairs with editing. Just be sure to phrase your offer correctly. Lead with, "I'm curious to learn more about your department. If you have any projects that need an extra hand, please let me know and I'd be happy to pitch in." Be sure to stay away from "I'm bored," "I have nothing to do," and "Get me out of here" language.

A few other ideas to explore when trying to bust your boredom:

- Take an online course – one that's provided by your company or something you want to learn/explore
- Read a pdf book on your computer
- Find a mentor or become a mentee

Boundaries

Setting new boundaries goes right in hand with downshifting – it is the perfect time to start creating your new normal. It is also time to make another big decision: what type of employee do you want to be during your love period (and beyond)? This is your chance to take a step back and re-enter your company fresh, but this time, you know exactly what you are getting yourself into!

Part of getting over the bumps in the road is figuring out why we keep hitting the same bumps, time after time. And most of it is our own fault – we have conditioned everyone around us to interact with us in a state of urgency or superstardom. Answering emails and calls at all hours, traveling everywhere just because you were asked to, and delivering just one more report before the deadline. When we enter a company, we do everything in our power to make a good impression and deliver top-notch work all of the time without realizing that we are setting ourselves up for our own downfall. It is difficult to change this because YOU need to change your actions and then reteach others your new normal.

Here are a few examples of how I have not only applied this for myself, but how I have also seen it in action:

I was an instant-email responder, among many other things. But I literally read every single email that I received and responded immediately before moving on to the next one. I was so quick to respond that people started getting worried if I hadn't gotten back to them with fifteen minutes (and no, I'm not exaggerating). I would get emails from my clients at all hours of the day and night, thanks to international travel and their own whacked out working standards, and I would always respond to them. And ironically enough, I could hardly ever get a response when I needed one… interesting dichotomy, no? When I was *done* with my job, I thought about the things that bugged me the most and the constant on-call via crackberry was at the top of my list. So one day, I left work ON TIME and turned my blackberry off when I stepped out of the doors. Off completely – ok, and I had to leave it in my car for the night. I definitely had some withdrawal symptoms for a while, but I felt amazing… I had my life back! And the less I responded at crazy hours, the fewer emails I received thus helping others resetting their own boundaries. Something very simple that vastly changed not only how I did my job, but also the expectations around my job.

In one of my least favorite jobs, my boss was calling me on my personal cell phone, on Saturday afternoons. He was at the park with his family and thought it was a great time to catch up with me and provide me with updates. Saturday's are not my favorite work days, especially when my job entails Monday through Friday hours and there were no pressing issues. After one too many Saturday's, I finally addressed this with my boss and let him know that he had interrupted my family time. We agreed upon a day and time that worked for us both going forward and also set a new precedent that he would only interrupt me on the weekend if the matter was urgent. Something small for both of us, but made my life much more enjoyable and helped me enjoy my time away from work without the fear of constantly being interrupted.

An example that I witnessed involved one of my clients. She was constantly traveling which led to less office time and therefore more issues overall. She said "yes: to every meeting that she was invited to, many of them international. She was constantly on the road attending meetings that were not always applicable and definitely not value-added for *her*. Add to the list that she had two young kids at home, and she was frustrated with her work/life non-balance. After chatting with her, I asked why she had to go to the meeting in Brussels and the convention in New York. She paused and then realized that she had the power to say "no" – or send someone else in her place if absolutely necessary. Holy crapoly, my friends – it was life changing. She reevaluated every meeting and travel offer from there on out – determining if her presence was absolutely necessary and weighed the outcomes. She cut back on her travel by 50% and her clients were as satisfied (if not more so) and her team was performing at a higher level than ever before.

Take one thing or action that you do that feels intrusive to you and your life – and reset the boundaries, NOW. And think big – there are more options on the table than you think. Can't stand the hours you work – ask your boss if you can adjust them. Want to work remote one day a week – ask if it is a possibility. Hate going to lunch with the team every week – stop going (unless it is mandatory). But more than the actual "thing" you are asking for, it is about YOU resetting the expectations for others so that over time, you will stop running into the same annoyances and create a more lasting love story.

Be Five Years Old Again

It does not matter how creative you think you are or if you consider yourself right- or left-brained. When you are falling back into your old ways at work, acting like you are five years old again will immediately impact your mood – and get you back on track. There was probably a time way back in the day that you colored at restaurants. Or maybe you did paint by numbers or danced up a storm or created mini-Hotwheels tracks. You did *something* creative when you were a kid and I bet you enjoyed it! And I also bet that you did not care who liked your end result, if there was a result at all, if it met anyone's standards, if it was creative enough, and so on.

You need a back-up creative plan to help you not only get back on track, but to also remind you about your goals. Nothing will jolt you more than a smile on your face. And remember that creativity is not about how good it is, for our purposes, it is simply to remind you that you are supposed to be enjoying life and falling back in love.

My creative outlet will be:

_____

"Find Your Passion"

Since you are committed to staying in your current role, you may or may not have made your work your passion. But you still need to have passion in your life – although my definition of passion may be radically different than what you are envisioning. For starters, I want you to think about things that you like to do outside of work – activities, motions, dreams, envies, and so on. You do not have to be madly obsessed with something for it to be considered a passion. And you do not need to be an expert in it either.

I used to be so paralyzed by perfection when it came to the activities I was "passionate" about, that I absolutely refused to participate in them – how ridiculous is that? If I could not deliver it perfectly, then I would not do anything at all. Denying something that made me smile, helped me learn, gave me something to look forward to outside of work, and consistently impacted my love (or lack thereof) for my job. The day that I hit such a big speed bump at work that I was not sure if I could ever get back on track, I took a walk with my camera in my hands. I had never done that before – but I allowed myself to snap pictures along the way and found myself smiling larger than I had in a long time.

As much as I'd like to tell you that you can compartmentalize work and your life, it takes a toll on you – particularly when one or the other is out of whack. Instead, they need to work harmoniously to ensure that you are getting the mental stimulation and fun that you need. If you are in a slump, challenge yourself to focus 20 minutes on something that you enjoy – and do it without criticism or judgment. And during your "passion time" thinking about your frustrations at work is off limits.

Fight Fair

When you are fighting with someone you care about, you typically let that person get away with a ton before finally ending the relationship, if you ever do. But with work, it seems as though we have higher expectations of the job than we have with our relationships outside of work. I know that I will move heaven and earth to resolve an argument with someone else – I will pull out all of the stops, not give up, and bite my tongue if I have to, just to settle things. But at work, we expect it to be easy sailing and at the first glimpse that it is not, we immediately say it isn't worth our time of effort. You are not fighting fair with your job.

I know, I know – your job is not an animate object that you can reason with, but you do have a "relationship" with it. Do you approach the various roadblocks along the way with your job, the same way you do with the people you love? For me, it was laughable how opposite my approach to both was – I was so willing to come to the table with people, but so ready to push work away. How do you handle quarrels with people you love? Are you applying the same love and care to your job when things pop up? I recommend putting a sticky note near your desk with the words "fight fair" on it, to remind you to give yourself a fighting chance at maintaining your relationship with your job through the rough times.

Happily Ever After... for now

(Sustainability)

- Accountability Partner
- Safety Zone
- Check-in Date Achievement

Happily Ever After... (for now)

If you have learned anything throughout this book, I hope it is that falling back in love with your job, and holding on to that love, takes ongoing and consistent work. And one of the most important lessons I want you to know is that you are creating your Happily Ever After – for now. Nothing lasts forever, nor should it. Know that this is your solution, for now. You are able to change your mind down the road, you may need to keep this portion of the book in front of you throughout your entire check-in date time period. That is ok – nothing is forever. And another helpful hint, sustainability is the hardest step, but can also be the most rewarding.

What's the Plan, Stan? Just because you are making progress towards your goals does not mean this will come easy to you. If you fail to plan, you plan to fail, right? And this is no different – we will be creating a sustainability plan to help you maintain and improve on the love you feel towards your job. We have already put a few components in place throughout this process, but we are not done yet.

Accountability Partner

My friend Jenny Blake introduced me to the concept of accountability partners. Sounds scary right – someone that you have to officially report into and will help hold you to your success? You know that friend that you told about your mission earlier – that was child's play compared to your accountability partner. Your accountability partner will be someone who will not only keep you on track and hold you accountable for staying on the right track, but he/she will also give you a swift kick in the butt when you fall off the horse. You have to pick the one friend you know will not let you get away with anything – you don't need a yes-man in this role. I warned you this was for real.

You may be certain that you do not need someone else to help keep you on track or hold you to your commitment to loving your job, but you are wrong. You will pick someone to be your accountability partner throughout this process and you will, at a minimum, provide them with weekly updates about your progress. I am notorious for not wanting to share things with an accountability partner (although I love having one), so here's what I found that has worked with me, just in case you are in the same boat.

I emailed one of my friends and asked her if she would become my accountability partner with the following: Hi – I am working towards falling in love with my job… I know, you can't wait for me to stop bitching and moaning about it. Which is why I need your help, if you're willing. I have committed to being engaged at my job and doing everything in my capability to have a positive outlook at work, until August 31, 2012 – the next 90 days. I need an accountability partner to help me stay on track and continue to make progress and sustain my results. Would you be willing to read one email a week that I send you letting you know about my progress? And if you see me waning, kick me in the butt?

Her response was awesome – she was excited to be a part of my change in attitude (maybe so she didn't have to listen to me complain all of the time?), and she was also happy to read one email a week. There was very little commitment for her to be a part of the process and I felt safe being honest and open with her about what was going on. It was a win-win for both of us.

My accountability partner is:

_____

Safety Zone

Sometimes you will just have a bad day... or a bad moment. And your accountability partner isn't necessarily the person you want to share that with in the immediate moment, you know – because they are there to swiftly kick you back into action. You need to create a safety zone where you can let loose and get everything off your chest in order to get back in the game.

<u>Fun Song and Dance</u>

I don't care who you are – doing a little dance at your desk will turn that frown immediately upside down. Pick out a song or two that is one of your favorites and always makes you smile and do a little dance, and put them in your ipod/phone, etc. so that you always have them with you in case of an emergency. I have a whole list of feel good songs just in case I run into an issue during the day. My list includes – "Just Dance" by Lady Gaga and anything by Pentatonix. When you run into an annoyance, your first stop should be your own song and dance; you may not need anything else to be back on track.

<u>Vent Buddy</u>

Get it out of your system. Choose another person than your accountability partner, to be your vent buddy. Pick someone who a) does not work with you, b) can let you share your experiences without negating them, and c) has been a supporter of you. This person will be your go-to person when you just need to vent. It happens, but instead of getting completely off track, allow yourself a few minutes to truly vent all of your frustrations out. Sometimes all you need is a little time blowing off some steam in order to feel brand new and recommitted.

Not sure you have someone who fits those requirements? Not a problem – don't hesitate to <u>send me a quick email</u> to vent and get it all out. And I'll be sure to help you get back on track as soon as you have aired all of your dirty laundry.

Supportive People Around You

You can be a lone wolf on this mission, but it is a lot harder to sustain (I tried, several times). One of the instant upgrades you can make that have a lasting impact, is being more careful about the people with whom you surround yourself – particularly at work. It is hard to stop being a Debbie Downer if everyone is gossiping and complaining at lunch or during coffee breaks. It is time to find yourself some new work friends – and the great part about this is that you have a completely clean slate. Similar to resetting boundaries, you have the opportunity to create new relationships where gossiping and negativity is not allowed. And all you have to do is to not bring anything negative up – people typically do not "trust" a new person enough to be the first to gossip, so just never open that door and you won't have to try and force that door closed at some point in the future.

You need to also be sure that the people around you at home are working with you, not against you. That they are fully on board with the love story you are trying to create. They may have been the person encouraging you to "hang in there," but they are also not used to the person you will become when you are happy at work. For many it is life changing – and very positive. But if you are surrounded by people who enjoy being Negative Nellies, then your transformation will be more difficult to adjust to. Have a realistic view of what to expect as you start changing your relationship with your job to ensure you are able to have the support and love of those around you to sustain your success.

Check-in Date Achievement

Yay – you have made it to your check-in date, or perhaps you're reading ahead to see what actually happens once you reach that date. The first thing you do is celebrate it – go big or go home. No really, regardless of what comes next, you absolutely must show some excitement and happiness – you have achieved a huge goal!

After the celebration, you have a few things you need to take care of immediately. Ask the following questions:

1. During the check-in date time period, how would I grade my commitment (A – F): _____

2. What I have learned about myself during this time period?
   _____

3. What have I achieved during this time? _____

4. How do I feel about where I am at with regards to my job? Am I in love, like, dislike, or done?

   _____

Your Grade

If you have given yourself anything lower than a C, you owe it to yourself to either fully commit to the process once more, or reevaluate what you should be doing with your career – perhaps your job just isn't salvageable at this time or it is time to cut your losses while you have your sanity and pick something else to fall in love with. Either way, get real about why you haven't passed your own test.

If you rated yourself an A or B – congratulations! I am so proud of you for fully committing to these steps and hanging in there to meet your check-in date. It takes a lot of effort and determination to do what you have done. You have given yourself ample opportunity to move forward and find even more success ahead.

Big Decision

If you gave yourself an A or B in reflection of this system, than you have a big decision to make. Since you used a short-term goal, you may or may not have reached your ultimate goal (whether it is a specific date, an earning amount, or so on). It's time to get real, and real fast. **Are you willing and able to fully commit to another check-in date?**

My personal scenario I shared with you early on about staying with a company due to a monetary contract clause? Well, I had to create three separate check-in dates to make it to the final date – nine months later, seriously. At the end of each check-in date period, I had to set a few hours aside on a weekend and determine my next step. I weighed all of the variables each time and made a determination about what was most important – the money, the experience, sticking in there, or moving forward. The funny thing was, after I made it to the first check-in date, I realized just how easy it was to go three months to reach a goal. It seemed like no time at all, my entire attitude had changed during the time period, and was content at work. Things still bothered me, but when they crept up, I was able to shake them off and keep my bigger picture in mind. Each time I realized not only was I *able* to recommit to another check-in date, but I wanted to!

You need to weigh your options for yourself – have you met your original objectives? Can you be fully committed again for another period of time? Have you had enough tools to keep you on track during the process? Have you learned enough to keep you engaged and moving forward? Is your personal balance scale, balanced? How in love are you with your job today? Do you want to be in love, or is it time to think about next steps and other options? Have I done everything in my capability to make this a success?

These are all valid questions – but the one that matters the most is: **am I willing to make the commitment again, to *this* job?**

What is Success?

Asking what success looks like is something that I typically need to know before I start any adventure – but with something so intangible, you should experience things that you never could have expected during this adventure. Looking back on everything that you have done during your check-in date, what does success look like and have you achieved it?

We have all experienced dates or relationships that seemed like a good idea at the time that ended up being disastrous. You know the saying "good on paper?" Falling back in love with your job could be just that – something that is good in theory, but not necessarily what you really want now that you have experienced it. And it is more than ok to change your mind at this fork in the road about your definition of success – but here's one thing to keep in mind. If you made it through your check-in date, learned something along the way, and gave it your all, regardless of your next decision – you have succeeded.

Get Your Ass in Gear Now

- Wrapping Up
- To-Do List

Get Your Ass in Gear Now

It is easy to be a bit overwhelmed looking back on the six steps to help you fall in love with your job (again). And instead of going into information overload, or getting stuck in analysis paralysis, here is the one thing that I want you to do right now to get you started: Pick your break-up (quit hating my job) date (when you are going to fully commit to this program). From there, the attached To Do sheet will help you along the way to ensure success and eternal (as eternal as you want it to be) love.

Wrapping Up

My hope is that after reading this book and completing the following To Do sheet that you will be on your path to being content, dare I say happy, at work. And along with your new frame of mind, I want you to firmly believe that your career path is fully in your hands – if you don't like something, you have the power and ability to change it, while always honoring your values and keeping your motivating factors in balance. Above all, work is not something you dread any longer; it is a source of enrichment and enlightenment – providing you the mental time and space to explore the many other passions in your life.

To Do List

- ❑ Quit Date: I fully commit to shift my mindset and be open to follow the guidance in this book on _____.
- ❑ I Hate My Job brainstorm: use this <u>handy template</u>
- ❑ My top two disharmony dimensions are: _____ and _____
- ❑ Tell my support network that I am going to work on falling in love with my job again.
- ❑ Break-up activity
- ❑ Affirm: I am getting off the gravy train of discontent
- ❑ Acknowledge gravity issues
- ❑ My mantra is: _____
- ❑ Quit Date (just in case you skipped item 1): _____
- ❑ My outfit: determine your top two motivating factors/values _____ & _____
- ❑ My check-in smart goal is: _____
- ❑ My motivate me "pull" goal is: _____
- ❑ Attempt downshifting one thing and rezone boundaries
- ❑ Find my creative outlet and practice it
- ❑ Partner up: My accountability partner is _____ and my vent partner is _____
- ❑ Evaluate achievement and determine my next goal
- ❑ Tell friends about Loosen Your White Collar and share my experience with Melissa

Thank You!

And now I'd like to ask your help to spread the love:

1. If you have learned something from this book and have your own love story to tell, I want to hear about it! Please leave a comment on my site at <u>Loosen Your White Collar</u>.

2. If you know of anyone who desperately needs to fall back in love with their job, please tell them about to visit Loosen Your White Collar to <u>sign-up for my free newsletter</u> and to <u>learn more about the book</u>.

Full of love,
Melissa

e: <u>melissa@loosenyourwhitecollar.com</u>
w: <u>http://loosenyourwhitecollar.com</u>
t: <u>@mellymelanz</u>
f: <u>http://facebook.com/loosenyourwhitecollar</u>

84601436R00035

Made in the USA
Columbia, SC
17 December 2017